50 Best French Cheese Recipes

By: Kelly Johnson

Table of Contents

- Croque Monsieur
- Quiche Lorraine
- Tartiflette
- Raclette
- Soupe à l'oignon (French onion soup)
- Cheese Soufflé
- Camembert au Four (Baked Camembert)
- Gratin Dauphinois
- Fondue Savoyarde
- Salade de Chèvre Chaud (Warm Goat Cheese Salad)
- Crottin de Chavignol Salad
- Tarte au Fromage (Cheese Tart)
- Fromage Blanc with Honey and Nuts
- Baked Brie with Garlic and Rosemary
- Cheese and Charcuterie Board
- Cordon Bleu
- Aligot (Cheesy Mashed Potatoes)

- Camembert and Apple Tart
- Bleu Cheese and Walnut Salad
- Cheese-stuffed Chicken Breast
- Croissant aux Fromages (Cheese Croissant)
- Raclette Sandwich
- Cheese and Herb Omelette
- Soufflé au Roquefort
- Chausson au Fromage (Cheese Turnover)
- Pissaladière with Cheese
- Cheese and Mushroom Crepes
- Tartine au Fromage (Cheese Toast)
- Cheese-stuffed Mushrooms
- Brie and Fig Tart
- Croquettes au Fromage (Cheese Croquettes)
- Cheese and Spinach Quiche
- Grilled Cheese with Comté
- Cheese-stuffed Meatballs
- Roquefort Dressing Salad
- Cheese and Potato Galette

- Raclette Pizza
- Baked Camembert with Cranberries
- Cheese-stuffed Zucchini
- Brie and Caramelized Onion Tart
- Cheese and Herb Puff Pastry
- Gougères (Cheese Puffs)
- Cheese and Tomato Tart
- Blue Cheese and Pear Salad
- Cheese-stuffed Bell Peppers
- Cheddar and Apple Tart
- Cheese and Leek Gratin
- Cheese-stuffed Ravioli
- Cheese and Ham Croissant
- Cheese and Herb Frittata

Croque Monsieur

Ingredients:

- 8 slices of white bread
- 4 slices of ham
- 4 slices of Gruyère cheese (or Emmental)
- 2 tbsp butter
- 2 tbsp all-purpose flour
- 1 cup milk
- 1 tsp Dijon mustard
- Salt and pepper

Instructions:

1. Preheat oven to 375°F (190°C).
2. Make béchamel sauce: Melt butter in a saucepan, stir in flour and cook 1-2 minutes. Slowly whisk in milk until thickened. Season with salt, pepper, and mustard.
3. Lightly toast the bread slices.
4. On 4 slices, layer ham and cheese, then top with the other bread slices.
5. Place sandwiches on a baking sheet, spread béchamel sauce on top and sprinkle extra cheese.
6. Bake 10-15 minutes until golden and bubbly. Serve hot.

Quiche Lorraine

Ingredients:

- 1 pie crust (store-bought or homemade)
- 6 slices bacon, chopped
- 1 cup shredded Gruyère cheese
- 3 large eggs
- 1 1/4 cups heavy cream
- Salt, pepper, and pinch of nutmeg

Instructions:

1. Preheat oven to 375°F (190°C).
2. Cook bacon until crisp, drain on paper towels.
3. Place pie crust in a tart pan, prick base with a fork.
4. Spread bacon and cheese evenly over crust.
5. Whisk eggs, cream, salt, pepper, and nutmeg. Pour into crust.
6. Bake 35-40 minutes until set and golden. Cool slightly before serving.

Tartiflette

Ingredients:

- 2 lbs (900 g) potatoes, peeled and sliced
- 1 onion, sliced
- 8 oz (225 g) bacon lardons
- 1/2 cup white wine
- 1 Reblochon cheese (about 14 oz or 400 g)
- Salt and pepper

Instructions:

1. Preheat oven to 375°F (190°C).
2. Boil potatoes in salted water until just tender, drain.
3. In a pan, cook bacon until crispy, add onions and cook until soft.
4. Add white wine, simmer until reduced.
5. Layer potatoes and bacon mixture in a baking dish.
6. Cut Reblochon in half horizontally, place rind-side up on top.
7. Bake 20 minutes until cheese is melted and golden. Serve hot.

Raclette

Ingredients:

- Raclette cheese (about 7 oz / 200 g per person)
- Boiled small potatoes
- Pickles (cornichons)
- Cured meats (ham, salami, etc.)
- Optional: steamed vegetables (broccoli, mushrooms)

Instructions:

1. Boil potatoes until tender.
2. Heat raclette cheese using a raclette grill or oven until melted and bubbly.
3. Serve melted cheese over potatoes, with pickles and cured meats on the side.
4. Enjoy as a communal dish.

Soupe à l'oignon (French Onion Soup)

Ingredients:

- 4 large onions, thinly sliced
- 3 tbsp butter
- 1 tsp sugar
- 2 cloves garlic, minced
- 6 cups beef broth
- 1/2 cup dry white wine (optional)
- 1 tbsp flour
- Salt and pepper
- Baguette slices
- 1 1/2 cups grated Gruyère cheese

Instructions:

1. Melt butter in a large pot. Add onions and sugar; cook slowly, stirring often, until caramelized (about 30-40 minutes).
2. Add garlic and cook 1 minute. Sprinkle flour, cook 2 minutes.
3. Add broth and wine, bring to boil, then simmer 20 minutes. Season.
4. Ladle soup into oven-safe bowls, top with baguette slices and grated cheese.
5. Broil until cheese is melted and golden. Serve immediately.

Cheese Soufflé

Ingredients:

- 3 tbsp butter
- 3 tbsp all-purpose flour
- 1 cup milk
- 4 eggs, separated
- 1 1/2 cups grated Gruyère cheese
- Salt, pepper, and pinch of nutmeg

Instructions:

1. Preheat oven to 375°F (190°C). Butter a soufflé dish and sprinkle with cheese.
2. Make béchamel: melt butter, stir in flour, cook 1-2 minutes. Whisk in milk until thickened.
3. Remove from heat, stir in egg yolks, cheese, seasoning.
4. Beat egg whites until stiff peaks form, gently fold into the cheese mixture.
5. Pour into dish, bake 25-30 minutes until puffed and golden. Serve immediately.

Camembert au Four (Baked Camembert)

Ingredients:

- 1 whole Camembert cheese (in wooden box)
- 1-2 garlic cloves, thinly sliced
- Fresh rosemary sprigs
- Drizzle of olive oil
- Baguette for dipping

Instructions:

1. Preheat oven to 350°F (175°C).
2. Remove Camembert from plastic, place back in wooden box or in a small ovenproof dish.
3. Score the top of cheese, insert garlic slices and rosemary. Drizzle with olive oil.
4. Bake 15-20 minutes until soft and gooey inside.
5. Serve warm with fresh baguette.

Gratin Dauphinois

Ingredients:

- 2 lbs (900 g) potatoes, thinly sliced
- 2 cups heavy cream
- 1 garlic clove, halved
- 1 cup grated Gruyère cheese
- Salt, pepper, and a pinch of nutmeg
- Butter for greasing

Instructions:

1. Preheat oven to 350°F (175°C).
2. Rub a baking dish with garlic and butter it well.
3. Layer potatoes evenly in the dish, seasoning each layer with salt, pepper, and nutmeg.
4. Pour cream over potatoes and top with grated cheese.
5. Bake 1 hour or until potatoes are tender and top is golden and bubbling. Let rest a few minutes before serving.

Fondue Savoyarde

Ingredients:

- 200g Gruyère cheese, grated
- 200g Comté cheese, grated
- 100g Emmental cheese, grated
- 1 garlic clove, halved
- 300ml dry white wine
- 1 tsp lemon juice
- 1 tbsp cornstarch
- 3 tbsp kirsch (cherry brandy), optional
- Freshly ground black pepper and nutmeg
- Cubed crusty bread for dipping

Instructions:

1. Rub the inside of a fondue pot with garlic, then discard the garlic.
2. Heat white wine and lemon juice in the pot until hot but not boiling.
3. Toss grated cheeses with cornstarch. Gradually add cheese to the wine, stirring constantly until melted and smooth.
4. Stir in kirsch (if using), season with pepper and a pinch of nutmeg.
5. Keep warm on low heat. Dip bread cubes into the melted cheese with fondue forks.

Salade de Chèvre Chaud (Warm Goat Cheese Salad)

Ingredients:

- Mixed salad greens
- 4 small rounds of goat cheese (Chèvre)
- 4 slices of baguette
- Olive oil
- Honey (optional)
- Walnuts or pecans
- Balsamic vinaigrette

Instructions:

1. Preheat oven to 375°F (190°C).
2. Place goat cheese rounds on baguette slices on a baking sheet, drizzle with olive oil and a little honey if you like.
3. Bake 8-10 minutes until cheese is melted and golden.
4. Toss salad greens with vinaigrette, top with nuts.
5. Place warm goat cheese toasts on salad and serve immediately.

Crottin de Chavignol Salad

Ingredients:

- Mixed greens or frisée
- 4 Crottin de Chavignol goat cheeses (small rounds)
- Olive oil
- Honey
- Walnuts
- Baguette slices
- Balsamic vinegar or vinaigrette

Instructions:

1. Preheat oven to 375°F (190°C).
2. Place Crottin cheese on baguette slices, drizzle with honey and olive oil.
3. Bake 8-10 minutes until cheese is bubbling and golden.
4. Toss greens with vinaigrette and walnuts.
5. Top salad with warm Crottin toasts and serve.

Tarte au Fromage (Cheese Tart)

Ingredients:

- 1 sheet puff pastry or shortcrust pastry
- 200g soft cheese (e.g., cream cheese, ricotta, or Neufchâtel)
- 100g grated cheese (Gruyère or Emmental)
- 2 eggs
- 100ml cream
- Salt and pepper
- Fresh herbs (thyme, chives) optional

Instructions:

1. Preheat oven to 375°F (190°C).
2. Line a tart pan with pastry, prick base with fork.
3. Whisk eggs and cream with soft cheese, season well.
4. Stir in grated cheese and herbs if using.
5. Pour filling into tart shell.
6. Bake 30-35 minutes until set and golden. Cool slightly before serving.

Fromage Blanc with Honey and Nuts

Ingredients:

- 1 cup fromage blanc (or plain Greek yogurt as substitute)
- 2 tbsp honey
- A handful of mixed nuts (walnuts, almonds, hazelnuts), roughly chopped

Instructions:

1. Spoon fromage blanc into bowls.
2. Drizzle with honey.
3. Sprinkle chopped nuts on top.
4. Serve as a simple dessert or breakfast.

Baked Brie with Garlic and Rosemary

Ingredients:

- 1 wheel of Brie cheese
- 2 garlic cloves, thinly sliced
- 2 sprigs fresh rosemary
- Drizzle of olive oil
- Crackers or baguette slices

Instructions:

1. Preheat oven to 350°F (175°C).
2. Score the top of the Brie with a knife, tuck garlic slices and rosemary sprigs into the cuts.
3. Drizzle olive oil over the top.
4. Bake for 15-20 minutes until soft and melty.
5. Serve warm with crackers or bread.

Cheese and Charcuterie Board

Ingredients:

- Variety of cheeses (e.g., Brie, Camembert, Comté, Roquefort, Goat cheese)
- Assortment of cured meats (e.g., saucisson, prosciutto, ham)
- Fresh and dried fruits (grapes, figs, apricots)
- Nuts (almonds, walnuts)
- Olives and cornichons
- Crackers and sliced baguette
- Honey or fig jam

Instructions:

1. Arrange cheeses, meats, fruits, nuts, and accompaniments artistically on a large wooden board or platter.
2. Provide small knives for each cheese and bowls for olives and jams.
3. Enjoy as a casual appetizer or party platter.

Cordon Bleu

Ingredients:

- 4 chicken breasts, pounded thin
- 4 slices ham
- 4 slices Swiss cheese (Gruyère or Emmental)
- 1 cup flour
- 2 eggs, beaten
- 1 1/2 cups breadcrumbs
- Salt and pepper
- Butter or oil for frying

Instructions:

1. Preheat oven to 350°F (175°C).
2. Place a slice of ham and cheese on each chicken breast, roll up and secure with toothpicks.
3. Season flour with salt and pepper.
4. Dredge each roll in flour, then egg, then breadcrumbs.
5. Brown in butter or oil over medium heat until golden on all sides.
6. Transfer to oven and bake 15-20 minutes until cooked through.
7. Remove toothpicks and serve hot.

Aligot (Cheesy Mashed Potatoes)

Ingredients:

- 2 lbs (900g) potatoes, peeled and cubed
- 1 cup crème fraîche or heavy cream
- 2 tbsp butter
- 8 oz (225g) Tomme cheese or mozzarella (for stretchiness)
- 2 garlic cloves, minced
- Salt and pepper

Instructions:

1. Boil potatoes until tender, then drain.
2. In a pot, warm cream, butter, and garlic until butter melts.
3. Mash potatoes, then gradually mix in cream mixture.
4. Add cheese and stir vigorously over low heat until melted and stretchy.
5. Season with salt and pepper and serve immediately.

Camembert and Apple Tart

Ingredients:

- 1 sheet puff pastry
- 1 Camembert cheese wheel, sliced
- 2 apples, thinly sliced
- 1 tbsp honey
- Fresh thyme
- Optional: crushed walnuts

Instructions:

1. Preheat oven to 375°F (190°C).
2. Lay puff pastry on a baking sheet, score a 1-inch border around edges.
3. Arrange apple slices inside the border, layer Camembert slices on top.
4. Drizzle with honey and sprinkle thyme (and walnuts if using).
5. Fold edges over slightly and bake 25-30 minutes until golden and bubbly.

Bleu Cheese and Walnut Salad

Ingredients:

- Mixed greens or arugula
- 1/2 cup crumbled blue cheese
- 1/2 cup walnuts, toasted
- Sliced pears or apples (optional)
- Balsamic vinaigrette

Instructions:

1. Toss greens with vinaigrette.
2. Top with blue cheese, walnuts, and fruit slices if using.
3. Serve immediately.

Cheese-stuffed Chicken Breast

Ingredients:

- 4 chicken breasts
- 4 oz (115g) soft cheese (goat cheese, cream cheese, or mozzarella)
- Fresh herbs (parsley, thyme, or basil)
- Salt and pepper
- Olive oil

Instructions:

1. Preheat oven to 375°F (190°C).
2. Slice a pocket into each chicken breast.
3. Mix cheese with herbs, salt, and pepper; stuff into pockets.
4. Secure with toothpicks, season outside.
5. Sear chicken in olive oil until golden, then finish baking 20 minutes until cooked through.

Croissant aux Fromages (Cheese Croissant)

Ingredients:

- 1 sheet puff pastry or ready croissant dough
- 1/2 cup grated Gruyère or Emmental cheese
- 1 egg, beaten (for egg wash)

Instructions:

1. Preheat oven to 375°F (190°C).
2. Roll out dough, cut into triangles.
3. Sprinkle cheese on each triangle, roll up from wide end to tip.
4. Brush with egg wash, bake 12-15 minutes until golden.
5. Serve warm.

Raclette Sandwich

Ingredients:

- Rustic bread or baguette
- Slices of raclette cheese
- Cooked ham or cured meat
- Pickles (cornichons)
- Butter

Instructions:

1. Butter bread slices, layer ham and raclette cheese.
2. Grill or toast sandwich until cheese melts and bread is crisp.
3. Serve with pickles on the side.

Cheese and Herb Omelette

Ingredients:

- 3 eggs
- 1/4 cup grated cheese (Gruyère, Emmental, or goat cheese)
- Fresh herbs (chives, parsley, tarragon)
- Salt and pepper
- Butter

Instructions:

1. Beat eggs with salt, pepper, and chopped herbs.
2. Melt butter in pan over medium heat.
3. Pour eggs in, cook gently until almost set.
4. Sprinkle cheese, fold omelette and cook 1-2 minutes until cheese melts.
5. Serve immediately.

Soufflé au Roquefort

Ingredients:

- 3 tbsp butter
- 3 tbsp flour
- 1 cup milk
- 4 eggs, separated
- 100g Roquefort cheese, crumbled
- Salt and pepper

Instructions:

1. Preheat oven to 375°F (190°C). Butter soufflé dish and dust with flour.
2. Make béchamel: melt butter, stir in flour, cook 1-2 minutes. Whisk in milk until thickened.
3. Remove from heat, stir in egg yolks and Roquefort. Season lightly.
4. Beat egg whites to stiff peaks, fold carefully into cheese mixture.
5. Pour into dish, bake 25-30 minutes until puffed and golden. Serve immediately.

Chausson au Fromage (Cheese Turnover)

Ingredients:

- 1 sheet puff pastry
- 1 cup grated cheese (Gruyère, Emmental, or Comté)
- 1 small onion, finely chopped and sautéed (optional)
- 1 egg, beaten (for egg wash)

Instructions:

1. Preheat oven to 375°F (190°C).
2. Cut puff pastry into squares (about 4-5 inches).
3. Mix cheese with sautéed onion if using.
4. Place a spoonful of cheese mixture in the center of each square.
5. Fold pastry over to form a triangle, press edges to seal.
6. Brush with egg wash.
7. Bake 15-20 minutes until golden and puffed. Serve warm.

Pissaladière with Cheese

Ingredients:

- 1 pizza dough or bread dough base
- 3 large onions, thinly sliced
- 2 tbsp olive oil
- 1 tsp dried thyme
- 2 tbsp black olives (optional)
- 1/2 cup grated cheese (Gruyère or Emmental)

Instructions:

1. Preheat oven to 400°F (200°C).
2. Sauté onions in olive oil on low heat until caramelized (about 30 minutes). Add thyme and season.
3. Roll out dough on baking sheet. Spread onions evenly on top.
4. Sprinkle cheese and olives over onions.
5. Bake 15-20 minutes until crust is golden and cheese melted. Serve warm.

Cheese and Mushroom Crepes

Ingredients:

- 6 crepes (store-bought or homemade)
- 2 cups mushrooms, sliced
- 1 tbsp butter
- 1 cup grated Gruyère cheese
- 1 clove garlic, minced
- Salt and pepper
- Fresh parsley for garnish

Instructions:

1. Sauté mushrooms and garlic in butter until soft, season.
2. Fill each crepe with mushrooms and cheese.
3. Fold or roll crepes, place in a buttered baking dish.
4. Sprinkle extra cheese on top.
5. Bake at 350°F (175°C) for 10-15 minutes until cheese melts. Garnish with parsley.

Tartine au Fromage (Cheese Toast)

Ingredients:

- Rustic bread slices
- Butter
- 1 cup grated cheese (Gruyère, Comté, or goat cheese)
- Fresh herbs (thyme, chives)
- Optional: sliced tomatoes or mustard

Instructions:

1. Preheat broiler or oven grill.
2. Butter bread slices lightly.
3. Top with cheese and herbs (add tomatoes or a thin mustard spread if desired).
4. Broil until cheese melts and turns golden. Serve immediately.

Cheese-stuffed Mushrooms

Ingredients:

- 12 large button mushrooms, stems removed
- 1/2 cup cream cheese or goat cheese
- 1/4 cup grated Parmesan or Gruyère
- 1 clove garlic, minced
- Fresh parsley, chopped
- Salt and pepper

Instructions:

1. Preheat oven to 375°F (190°C).
2. Mix cheeses with garlic, parsley, salt, and pepper.
3. Stuff mushroom caps with cheese mixture.
4. Place on baking sheet, bake 15-20 minutes until golden and bubbly. Serve warm.

Brie and Fig Tart

Ingredients:

- 1 sheet puff pastry
- 1 wheel Brie cheese, sliced
- 6-8 fresh figs, sliced (or use fig jam)
- 1 tbsp honey
- Fresh thyme or rosemary

Instructions:

1. Preheat oven to 375°F (190°C).
2. Roll puff pastry on baking sheet.
3. Arrange Brie slices and fig slices (or dollops of fig jam) on pastry.
4. Drizzle honey and sprinkle herbs on top.
5. Bake 25-30 minutes until pastry is golden and cheese melted. Serve warm.

Croquettes au Fromage (Cheese Croquettes)

Ingredients:

- 1 cup mashed potatoes or béchamel sauce thickened
- 1 cup grated cheese (Gruyère, Emmental)
- 2 eggs, beaten
- 1 cup breadcrumbs
- Oil for frying

Instructions:

1. Mix cheese into mashed potatoes or béchamel, cool mixture.
2. Shape into small cylinders or balls.
3. Dip in egg, then coat with breadcrumbs.
4. Fry in hot oil until golden brown. Drain on paper towels. Serve hot.

Cheese and Spinach Quiche

Ingredients:

- 1 pie crust
- 200g fresh spinach, wilted and drained
- 1 cup grated cheese (Gruyère or Swiss)
- 3 eggs
- 1 cup cream or milk
- Salt, pepper, and nutmeg

Instructions:

1. Preheat oven to 375°F (190°C).
2. Line a tart pan with pie crust, prick base.
3. Spread spinach and cheese evenly in crust.
4. Whisk eggs, cream, salt, pepper, and nutmeg; pour over spinach.
5. Bake 30-35 minutes until set and golden. Cool slightly before serving.

Grilled Cheese with Comté

Ingredients:

- 4 slices of rustic bread
- 200g Comté cheese, sliced
- Butter

Instructions:

1. Butter one side of each bread slice.
2. Place cheese between two slices, buttered sides out.
3. Heat a skillet over medium heat, grill sandwich until golden and cheese is melted, about 3-4 minutes per side. Serve warm.

Cheese-stuffed Meatballs

Ingredients:

- 500g ground beef or mixed beef and pork
- 1 cup breadcrumbs
- 1 egg
- 100g cheese cubes (Gruyère, mozzarella, or Comté)
- 2 cloves garlic, minced
- Salt and pepper
- Olive oil for frying

Instructions:

1. Mix meat, breadcrumbs, egg, garlic, salt, and pepper.
2. Form small patties, place cheese cube in center, cover with more meat and seal well.
3. Fry meatballs in olive oil until browned all over and cooked through. Serve hot.

Roquefort Dressing Salad

Ingredients:

- 100g Roquefort cheese, crumbled
- 3 tbsp mayonnaise
- 2 tbsp sour cream or Greek yogurt
- 1 tbsp lemon juice or white wine vinegar
- Salt and pepper
- Mixed greens or iceberg lettuce

Instructions:

1. Mix Roquefort, mayo, sour cream, and lemon juice until creamy.
2. Season with salt and pepper.
3. Toss dressing with salad greens and serve.

Cheese and Potato Galette

Ingredients:

- 4 medium potatoes, peeled and thinly sliced
- 1 cup grated cheese (Gruyère or Comté)
- 2 tbsp butter
- Salt and pepper
- Fresh thyme or rosemary

Instructions:

1. Preheat oven to 375°F (190°C).
2. Butter a round ovenproof skillet or dish.
3. Layer potato slices, sprinkle cheese, herbs, salt, and pepper. Repeat layers.
4. Dot with butter. Cover with foil and bake 40 minutes.
5. Remove foil and bake 10-15 more minutes until golden and crispy.

Pizza

Ingredients:

- 1 pizza dough base
- 150g raclette cheese, sliced
- 100g cooked potatoes, thinly sliced
- 50g cooked bacon or ham
- Caramelized onions
- Fresh arugula (optional)

Instructions:

1. Preheat oven to 450°F (230°C).
2. Roll out dough on pizza stone or tray.
3. Spread caramelized onions, then layer potatoes, bacon, and raclette cheese.
4. Bake 12-15 minutes until crust is golden and cheese melted.
5. Top with fresh arugula before serving if desired.

Baked Camembert with Cranberries

Ingredients:

- 1 whole Camembert cheese
- 3 tbsp cranberry sauce or fresh cranberries
- 1 tsp fresh thyme
- Honey (optional)
- Crackers or sliced baguette

Instructions:

1. Preheat oven to 350°F (175°C).
2. Place Camembert in a small baking dish or its wooden box (without plastic).
3. Top with cranberry sauce and thyme. Drizzle honey if you like.
4. Bake 15-20 minutes until melted inside. Serve warm with bread or crackers.

Cheese-stuffed Zucchini

Ingredients:

- 4 medium zucchinis, halved and hollowed
- 1 cup ricotta or cream cheese
- 1/2 cup grated Parmesan or Gruyère
- 1 garlic clove, minced
- Fresh herbs (basil, parsley)
- Salt and pepper
- Olive oil

Instructions:

1. Preheat oven to 375°F (190°C).
2. Mix cheeses, garlic, herbs, salt, and pepper.
3. Fill zucchini halves with cheese mixture.
4. Drizzle with olive oil and bake 20-25 minutes until zucchini is tender and top is golden.

Brie and Caramelized Onion Tart

Ingredients:

- 1 sheet puff pastry
- 1 wheel Brie cheese, sliced
- 2 large onions, thinly sliced
- 2 tbsp butter
- 1 tbsp olive oil
- 1 tsp sugar
- Fresh thyme

Instructions:

1. Preheat oven to 375°F (190°C).
2. Caramelize onions in butter and olive oil with sugar over low heat until golden and soft (~30 minutes).
3. Roll puff pastry on baking sheet. Spread caramelized onions evenly.
4. Top with Brie slices and sprinkle thyme.
5. Bake 25-30 minutes until pastry is golden and cheese melted.

Cheese and Herb Puff Pastry

Ingredients:

- 1 sheet puff pastry
- 1 cup grated cheese (Gruyère, Comté, or Emmental)
- 2 tbsp chopped fresh herbs (parsley, chives, tarragon)
- 1 egg, beaten (for egg wash)

Instructions:

1. Preheat oven to 375°F (190°C).
2. Roll out puff pastry and sprinkle cheese and herbs evenly over half.
3. Fold pastry over, seal edges, and cut into shapes or strips.
4. Brush with egg wash and bake 15-20 minutes until golden and puffed. Serve warm.

Gougères (Cheese Puffs)

Ingredients:

- 1/2 cup water
- 1/2 cup milk
- 1/2 cup unsalted butter
- 1 cup all-purpose flour
- 4 eggs
- 1 cup grated Gruyère cheese
- Salt and pepper

Instructions:

1. Preheat oven to 425°F (220°C).
2. In a saucepan, combine water, milk, butter, and a pinch of salt; bring to a boil.
3. Remove from heat, add flour all at once, stir vigorously until dough forms and pulls away from sides.
4. Return to low heat and cook 1-2 minutes, stirring to dry dough slightly.
5. Transfer dough to a bowl; beat in eggs one at a time until smooth.
6. Fold in cheese and season with pepper.
7. Pipe or spoon small mounds onto a baking sheet lined with parchment.
8. Bake 20-25 minutes until puffed and golden. Serve warm.

Cheese and Tomato Tart

Ingredients:

- 1 sheet puff pastry or shortcrust pastry
- 3-4 ripe tomatoes, sliced
- 1 cup grated cheese (Gruyère, Comté, or mozzarella)
- 1 tbsp Dijon mustard
- Fresh basil or thyme
- Salt and pepper

Instructions:

1. Preheat oven to 375°F (190°C).
2. Roll out pastry, prick with fork, and blind bake 10 minutes.
3. Spread mustard over pastry base.
4. Layer cheese and tomato slices, season with salt, pepper, and herbs.
5. Bake 20-25 minutes until pastry is golden and cheese melted.

Blue Cheese and Pear Salad

Ingredients:

- Mixed salad greens
- 1 ripe pear, thinly sliced
- 1/2 cup crumbled blue cheese
- 1/4 cup toasted walnuts
- Balsamic vinaigrette

Instructions:

1. Toss greens with vinaigrette.
2. Top with pear slices, blue cheese, and walnuts. Serve immediately.

Cheese-stuffed Bell Peppers

Ingredients:

- 4 bell peppers, tops cut off and seeds removed
- 1 cup cooked rice or quinoa
- 1 cup shredded cheese (Mozzarella, Gruyère, or Cheddar)
- 1/2 cup sautéed onions and garlic
- 1 tbsp fresh herbs (parsley, thyme)
- Salt and pepper

Instructions:

1. Preheat oven to 375°F (190°C).
2. Mix rice, cheese, sautéed onions, herbs, salt, and pepper.
3. Stuff mixture into peppers.
4. Place in baking dish, cover with foil, bake 30-35 minutes until peppers are tender and cheese melted.

Cheddar and Apple Tart

Ingredients:

- 1 sheet shortcrust pastry
- 2 apples, thinly sliced
- 1 cup shredded sharp Cheddar cheese
- 1 tbsp honey
- Fresh thyme

Instructions:

1. Preheat oven to 375°F (190°C).
2. Roll out pastry and place in tart pan.
3. Layer apples and cheese alternately.
4. Drizzle honey and sprinkle thyme.
5. Bake 30-35 minutes until golden and bubbling.

Cheese and Leek Gratin

Ingredients:

- 3 large leeks, cleaned and sliced
- 1 cup grated Gruyère or Emmental cheese
- 1 cup heavy cream
- 2 tbsp butter
- Salt, pepper, and nutmeg

Instructions:

1. Preheat oven to 375°F (190°C).
2. Sauté leeks in butter until soft.
3. Place leeks in gratin dish, season with salt, pepper, and nutmeg.
4. Pour cream over and top with cheese.
5. Bake 25-30 minutes until golden and bubbly.

Cheese-stuffed Ravioli

Ingredients:

- Fresh pasta dough (or store-bought)
- 1 cup ricotta cheese
- 1/2 cup grated Parmesan
- 1/4 cup chopped spinach (optional)
- Salt, pepper, and nutmeg

Instructions:

1. Mix ricotta, Parmesan, spinach, salt, pepper, and nutmeg.
2. Roll out pasta dough, place teaspoons of filling spaced evenly.
3. Cover with another sheet, press around filling to seal, cut ravioli.
4. Cook in boiling salted water 3-4 minutes until al dente. Serve with butter and sage or tomato sauce.

Cheese and Ham Croissant

Ingredients:

- 4 croissants (store-bought or homemade)
- 4 slices ham
- 1 cup grated cheese (Gruyère or Swiss)

Instructions:

1. Preheat oven to 350°F (175°C).
2. Slice croissants horizontally.
3. Layer ham and cheese inside.
4. Place on baking sheet and bake 10-12 minutes until cheese melts.

Cheese and Herb Frittata

Ingredients:

- 6 eggs
- 1/2 cup grated cheese (Parmesan, Gruyère, or feta)
- 1/4 cup chopped fresh herbs (parsley, chives, tarragon)
- Salt and pepper
- 1 tbsp olive oil

Instructions:

1. Preheat oven to 350°F (175°C).
2. Beat eggs with cheese, herbs, salt, and pepper.
3. Heat olive oil in ovenproof skillet, pour in egg mixture.
4. Cook on stove for 3-4 minutes until edges start to set.
5. Transfer skillet to oven and bake 10-12 minutes until set and lightly golden.